D1785069

God is love.

St John (I John 4:16)

Acknowledgments

We would like to thank all those who have given us permission to include material in this book. Every effort has been made to trace and acknowledge copyright holders of all the quotations in this book. We apologize for any errors or omissions that may remain, and would ask those concerned to contact the publishers, who will ensure that full acknowledgment is made in the future.

Extracts on pages 4, 6, 9, 19, 21, 27, 36, 42, 59 and 60 are taken from the New Revised Standard Version of the Bible, copyright © 1989 by the Division of Christian Education of the National Council of the Churches of Christ in the USA.

Extracts on pages 7, 10, 12, 16, 24, 25, 29, 30, 33, 34, 39, 40, 44, 45, 50, 53, 57, 62 and 63 are taken from the Revised Standard Version of the Bible, copyright © 1946, 1952, 1971 by the Division of Christian Education of the National Council of the Churches of Christ in the USA.

Extracts on pages 14, 38, 54, 55 and 59 are taken from the Good News Bible, published by the Bible Societies/HarperCollins Publishers Ltd UK © American Bible Society, 1966, 1971, 1976, 1992.

Extracts on pages 13, 31, 34, 35, 41, 47, 51 and 57 are taken from the Revised English Bible © 1989 by permission of Oxford and Cambridge University Presses.

Extracts on pages 10, 22 and 43 are based on the Authorized Version of the Bible (The King James Bible), the rights of which are vested in the Crown, and are reproduced by permission of the Crown's Patentee, Cambridge University Press.

Extracts on pages 18, 23, 47 and 48 are taken from the New Jerusalem Bible © 1985 by Darton, Longman and Todd Ltd and Doubleday and Company, Inc.

Extracts on pages 20, 28, 32 and 61 are taken from the Holy Bible, New International Version, copyright © 1973, 1978, 1984 by International Bible Society. Used by permission.

What does the Lord require of you but to do justice, and to love kindness, and to walk humbly with your God?

MICAH 6:8

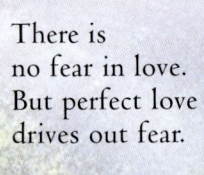

There is
no fear in love.
But perfect love
drives out fear.

St John (1 John 4:18)

Just as you do not know
how the breath comes to the
bones in the mother's womb,
so you do not know the work
of God, who makes everything.

Ecclesiastes 11:5

Whatever your hand
finds to do,
do with your might.

ECCLESIASTES 9:10

Being cheerful keeps you healthy.
It is slow death to be gloomy
all the time.

PROVERBS 17:22

The truth will make you free.

Jesus (John 8:32)

God has never been seen
by anyone, but if we love
one another, he himself dwells
in us; his love is brought to
perfection within us.

St John (1 John 4:12)

There are four things
that are too mysterious
for me to understand:
an eagle flying in the sky,
a snake moving on a rock,
a ship finding its way
over the sea, and a
man and a woman
falling in love.

PROVERBS 30:18–19

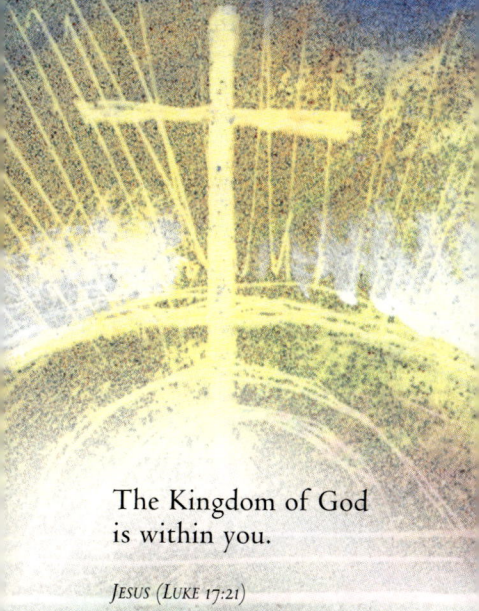

The Kingdom of God
is within you.

JESUS (LUKE 17:21)

God is spirit, and those who worship him must worship in spirit and truth.

JESUS (JOHN 4:24)

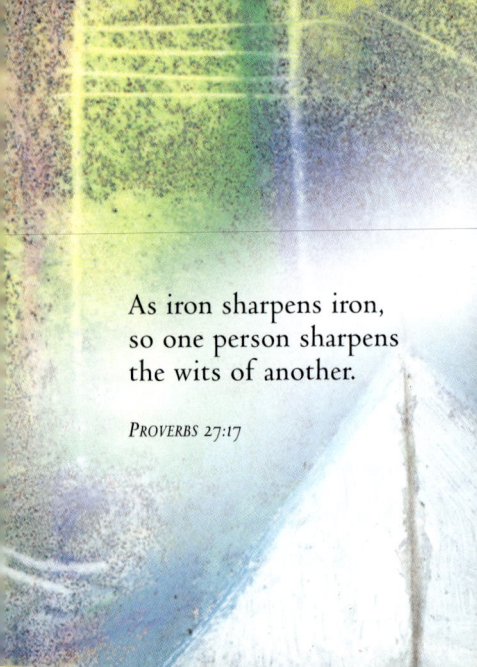

As iron sharpens iron,
so one person sharpens
the wits of another.

Proverbs 27:17

The love of money is
the root of all evils.

St Paul (I Timothy 6:10)

Whatever is true,
whatever is honourable,
whatever is just,
whatever is pure,
whatever is lovely,
whatever is gracious,
if there is any excellence,
if there is anything
worthy of praise,
think about these things.

St Paul (Philippians 4:8)

One who builds a lofty
entrance invites disaster.

PROVERBS 17:19

Let someone else
sing your praises,
but not your own mouth,
a stranger,
but not your own lips.

PROVERBS 27:2

To the pure all things are pure.

ST PAUL (TITUS 1:15)

He who meddles in a
quarrel not his own
is like one who takes a
passing dog by the ears.

PROVERBS 26:17

No one can serve two masters;
for either he will hate the one
and love the other, or he will be
devoted to one and despise
the other. You cannot serve
God and money.

JESUS (LUKE 16:13)

Clothe yourselves with compassion, kindness, humility, meekness, and patience. Bear with one another and, if anyone has a complaint against another, forgive each other… Above all, clothe yourselves with love, which binds everything together in perfect harmony.

St Paul

(Colossians 3:12–14)

Like a city breached and
defenceless is a man who
cannot control his temper.

PROVERBS 25:28

The wind blows where it pleases; you can hear its sound, but you cannot tell where it comes from or where it is going. So it is with everyone who is born of the Spirit.

JESUS (JOHN 3:8)

Every one who
exalts himself
will be humbled,
and he who
humbles himself
will be exalted.

JESUS (LUKE 14:11)

Singing to a
person who is
depressed is
like taking off
his clothes on a
cold day or like
rubbing salt
in a wound.

PROVERBS 25:20

Do not worry
about anything,
but in everything
by prayer and
supplication with
thanksgiving let
your requests be
made known
to God.

St Paul (Philippians 4:6)

Happiness lies more in
giving than in receiving.

Jesus (Acts 20:35)

Beware of all covetousness; for a man's life does not consist in the abundance of his possessions.

JESUS (LUKE 12:15)

Like clouds and wind
that bring no rain
is he who boasts of
gifts he never gives.

PROVERBS 25:14

The fruit of the Spirit is love,
joy, peace, patience, kindness,
goodness, faithfulness,
gentleness, self-control;
against such there is no law.

St Paul (*Galatians* 5:22)

Do not judge,
and you will not be judged.
Do not condemn,
and you will not be condemned.
Forgive, and you will be forgiven.
Give, and it will be given to you…
For with the measure you use,
it will be measured to you.

Jesus (Luke 6:37–38)

Unless a grain of wheat
falls into the ground and dies,
it remains that and nothing
more; but if it dies, it bears
a rich harvest.

Jesus (John 12:24)

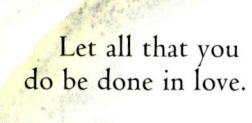

Let all that you
do be done in love.

St Paul (I Corinthians 16:14)

We brought nothing into the
world, and we cannot take
anything out of the world.

St Paul (I Timothy 6:7)

What good is it for a man
to gain the whole world,
yet forfeit his soul?

Jesus (Mark 8:36–37)

Love is patient; love is kind;
love is not envious or boastful
or arrogant or rude. It does not
insist on its own way; it is not
irritable or resentful; it does
not rejoice in wrongdoing, but
rejoices in the truth. It bears all
things, believes all things, hopes
all things, endures all things.
Love never ends.

St Paul (1 Corinthians 13:4–7)

'You shall love the Lord your God with all your heart, and with all your soul, and with all your mind.' This is the great and first commandment. And the second is like it: 'You shall love your neighbour as yourself.'

JESUS (MATTHEW 22:37–39)

The fear of the Lord is instruction in wisdom, and humility goes before honour.

PROVERBS 15:33

Unless you change
and become like
little children,
you will never
enter the
kingdom
of heaven.

JESUS
(MATTHEW 18:2–4)

Though I have
the gift of prophecy,
and understand all
mysteries, and all
knowledge; and though
I have all faith,
so that I could
remove mountains,
and have not love,
I am nothing.

St Paul

(I Corinthians 13: 2)

A soft answer turns away wrath,
but a harsh word stirs up anger.

PROVERBS 15:1

Do not repay anyone evil for evil… If it is possible, as far as it depends on you, live at peace with everyone.

St Paul (Romans 12:17)

Do to others as you would
have them do to you.

Jesus (Matthew 7:12)

The life of the body is
a tranquil heart, but envy is
a cancer in the bones.

PROVERBS 14:30

Rejoice with those who rejoice,
weep with those who weep.

St Paul (Romans 12:15)

Do not worry about tomorrow; it will have enough worries of its own. There is no need to add to the troubles each day brings.

JESUS (MATTHEW 6:34)

Gossip is sharp as a sword,
but the tongue of the wise
brings healing.

PROVERBS 12:18

Do not be conformed to this world but be transformed by the renewal of your mind.

ST PAUL (ROMANS 12:2)

Trust in the Lord with all your heart
and do not rely on your own insight.
In all your ways acknowledge him,
and he will make straight your paths

Proverbs 3:5–6

Blessed are the peacemakers:
for they shall be called
the children of God.

Jesus (Matthew 5:9)

Draw near to God,
and he will draw near to you.

St James (James 4:8)

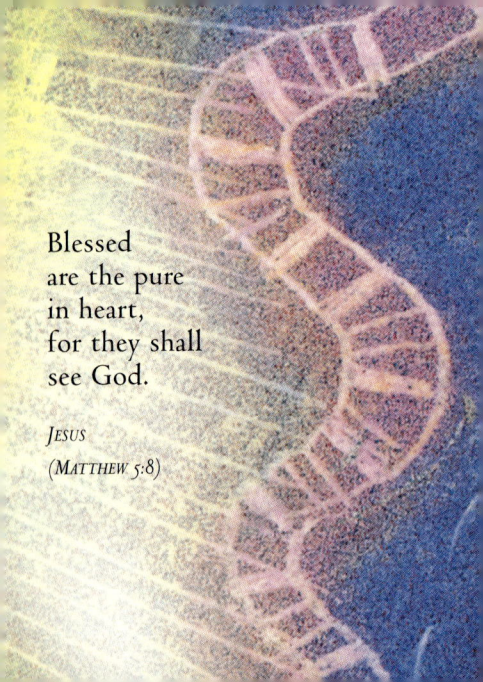

Blessed
are the pure
in heart,
for they shall
see God.

JESUS
(MATTHEW 5:8)

Be still
and know
that I am God.

PSALM 46:10

secrets of
wisdom

Compiled by
Philip Law

Illustrated by
Grahame Baker Smith

LION
Gifttimes

Be wise as serpents
and innocent as doves.

Jesus (Matthew 10:16)

secrets of
wisdom

This compilation copyright © 1999 Lion Publishing

Published by
Lion Publishing plc
Sandy Lane West, Oxford, England
ISBN 0 7459 4038 2

First edition 1999
10 9 8 7 6 5 4 3 2 1 0

A catalogue record for this book is available
from the British Library

Typeset in 12/12.5 Venetian 301
Printed and bound in Singapore